MW00605105

DISCOVER
the WORLD of
GROUND SQUIRRELS

©2019 HieroGraphics Books LLC
All Rights Reserved
No Unauthorized Copying,
Editing or Distribution

Photographic Images by Julia L. Wright ©2019
Cover Design by Julia L. Wright ©2019

TTerms of Use and Disclaimer:

No part of this book may be reproduced in whole or in part, or stored in a retrieval system or transmitted in any form or by any means electronic, recording, mechanical, photocopying or otherwise, without written permission of the publisher, except in the case of brief quotations embodied in critical articles or reviews.

The Author and Publisher have strived to be as accurate and complete as possible in the creation of this book. Due to the rapidly changing nature of climate conditions and information she does not warrant or represent at any time that all content within is still totally accurate. While all attempts have been made to verify information provided in this publication, the Author and Publisher assume no responsibility of liability for errors, omissions, or contrary interpretation of the subject matter herein.

The information presented in this book represents the view of the author as of the date of publication. The author reserves the right to alter and update opinions and information based upon new conditions and research. We have relied on our own experience as well as other sources for this book, and we have done our best to check facts and to give credit where it is due. In the event that any material is incorrect or has been used without proper permission, please contact us so that the oversight can be immediately corrected.

This book is presented for informational purposes only.

For information regarding permission, write to:
info@hierographicsbooksllc.com
Manitou Springs, CO

Printed in the United States of America
First Printing, January, 2019

ISBN-13: 978-0-9965816-3-9

DISCOVER the WORLD of GROUND SQUIRRELS

Illustrated Children's Book With Photos and Fun Facts About Ground Squirrels That Builds Kids Vocabulary

Julia L. Wright

HieroGraphics Books LLC

Unsplash contributor jehyun-sung

Table of Contents

Unsplash contributor eee2512

Introduction to "Discover the World of Ground Squirrels"

Some of my earliest childhood memories involve watching tree squirrels play in our wooded yard in northern Illinois. There were many trees that produced acorns and hickory nuts for them to eat and stash for the winter. And as I grew up, I never tired of watching squirrels at play wherever I lived.

When I moved to Colorado I was able to take hikes into the mountain wilderness where I have had many chances to observe some other varieties of tree squirrels in the wild and discovered their amusing little cousins, the chipmunk.

All the photographs in this book that are not accredited to someone else were taken by the author in Colorado. I hope these images will put a smile on all its readers' faces, both young and old.

I have been lucky to shoot some photographs of wild squirrels and a few chipmunks on my hikes. In the wild, they are much harder to catch on camera. The wild tree squirrels are very shy and wary of humans, so they prefer to dash away from humans rather than pose within sight.

Since I have never been so lucky as to be able to capture a prairie dog, marmot or any other species of ground squirrel with my camera, I am grateful for the great photographs I can share here thanks to others who shared them as public domain images.

Chipmunks are braver than most wild squirrels and will often come very close to humans expecting some food to be dropped on the ground. That means I have been able to take some fun and lovely photographs of a few of these very adorable creatures in the wilderness when hiking on various Colorado trails. Though, if I wasn't quick enough to take their pictures, or didn't offer them any food they were gone in an instant, dashing back to their homes or quickly hid deep in the surrounding vegetation.

On some of the more traveled hiking trails and around well established campgrounds, chipmunks can act very brave as they have come to feel very comfortable with having humans wandering and hiking through and camping in their woody and rocky habitats in the mountains and other wilderness areas.

My original "Discover the World of Squirrels" book that was attributed to my pen name of *Violet Burbach* only focused on presenting information about tree squirrels that live all over the world in every type of habitat. This book shares information about many varieties of ground-dwelling **Sciuridaes** that also live all around the world.

Ground-dwelling squirrels are very diverse members of the squirrel family. Their bodies vary in shape and they interact with each other in very different ways than tree squirrels do. Some can live in habitats where tree squirrels don't exist and have very different lifestyles.

As in the that book, this one also has a glossary of words that children reading this book may not be familiar with in their current vocabulary. When one of the words that can be found in the glossary appears, it will be brown in color.

We hope that you will spend some fun time with your kids who can have an enjoyable time learning some new words and interesting facts about these adorable furry creatures that live underground in almost every country around the world.

As a bonus lesson, you can find a free PDF to download with a simple word search and crossword puzzle using some glossary words at:
www.hierographicsbooksllc.com/squirrels-bonus/

Or you may chose to access a little PDF booklet that has more word searches and a crossword puzzle using the words in the glossary, plus it includes a few squirrel poems with simple illustrations and a squirrelly maze.

Unsplash contributor karen-lau

Welcome to the World of Ground Squirrels

What is your most favorite small wild creature to watch playing when out in wilderness areas?

Mine is the chipmunk, which I believe is the cutest member of the ground squirrel family.

I think most children will agree that chipmunks are one of the cutest wild creatures living in the forests and are often seen around campgrounds or on hiking trails.

Can you see the chipmunk hiding here?

Have you ever encountered a ground squirrel of any type?

Almost everyone, young and old, has at one time or another seen a chipmunk. And it can be very enjoyable to watch them when discovered in wilderness areas.

They can be very irresistible to look at and follow when you see them scampering across a rocky ledge or munching on plants next to a trail when you are hiking or camping.

Unsplash contributor emily-r

And if you have ever been lucky enough to see a marmot, I am sure that has made you smile and feel very privileged to meet one of these intriguing and very shy creatures.

Unsplash contributor eee2512

The only place I have ever seen a marmot was when traveling through or taking short hikes in Rocky Mountain National Park just outside of Estes Park in Colorado.

Squirrels have been around for a long, long time. Fossils of squirrels date back to about 35-40 million years ago. The oldest fossils look very similar to flying squirrels.

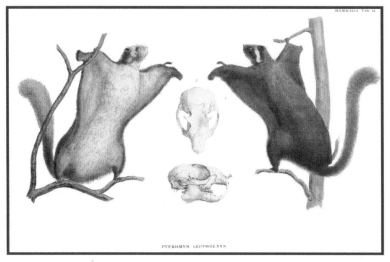

Wikipedia

The largest distribution of tree squirrels is found in North America. Here they are represented by a large and very diverse number of species and sub-species. All are refered to as the genus Tamias. It is believed that the common ancestor of all squirrels lived in North America.

Some North American ground-squirrels are migratory, and may be abundant in an area in one year, and then totally absent from there in the next year.

Unsplash contributor prashant-saini

The squirrel family includes many different types of squirrels. There are five subfamilies of living squirrels with 285 species. These includes tree squirrels, flying squirrels and ground squirrels, plus a few other types of rodents that aren't mentioned in this book.

This book is all about ground-dwelling squirrels, which includes chipmunks, ground squirrels, groundhogs/woodchucks, marmots and prairie dogs. Yes, one of the species in the family of ground squirrels is actually named *ground squirrel*. A bit confusing, but true.

Unsplash contributor matthew-essman

Squirrels can be found all over the planet in North and South America, Africa, Europe, Asia and Australia. They can be found living in almost every type of environment except the most northern and southern Polar Regions or extremely dry deserts. Some species of squirrels live in tropical rain forests, many live in wooded areas and a few species thrive in semi-arid deserts. The only place you will never encounter a ground squirrel is in Antarctica.

Although squirrels are wild creatures and usually live in the forests or mountainous regions most everywhere, many have become very comfortable living in residential or agricultural areas as they have become very comfortable around people.

Some people consider them pests, when they are discovered eating vegetables, fruits, berries or grains growing in a garden or around the edges of a farm.

Unsplash contributor john-d-eichenour

Squirrels come in many colors that can vary even within their own species. Many squirrels are a reddish brown in color, but some have gray or even black fur. Some have stripes, while others don't.

Unsplash contributor carlos-hernandez

As with most other mammals, communication among squirrels involves both vocalizations and posturing. Each species has quite a varied repertoire of sounds it makes, including low-pitched noises, squeaks, chattering, and raspy, almost purring sounds.

Unsplash contributor Andrea Schafthuizen

Typically, as with other squirrels, *except flying squirrels*, ground squirrels are mostly seen during the daytime and hide in their burrows during the dark night hours.

Every type of squirrel has rather large eyes, which gives them an excellent sense of vision. This is especially helpful for the tree-dwelling species. Most ground squirrels also have large eyes which helps them spot predators at far distances on the ground or circling high above them in the sky if they are living in very open areas, such as a desert or on a prairie.

Squirrels That Live On The Ground

The American landscape is full of variously sized mammals that scamper, burrow, or otherwise run about on the ground. These animals are most likely member of the Sciuridae ground squirrel family.

The name "ground squirrel" is typically applied to small rodents that excavate burrows and are associated with open habitats at temperate latitudes in North America and Eurasia, as well as tropical regions and arid regions of Africa. They can be found living in areas at sea level or high up in the mountains, in open habitats and occasionally in forests. But there are many other types of ground squirrels found around the world.

There are actually 62 species of these long-bodied ground-dwelling squirrels that are active during the day. Within this family each species varies in size and habitats. The largest subfamily of squirrels is the ground-living forms, which includes prairie dogs, ground squirrels, groundhogs/woodchucks, marmots and chipmunks.

Pixabay contributor artyangely

Grounds squirrels have many of the same characteristics, including diet and behavior. They have short legs, strong claws, small rounded ears, and a short or moderately long tail.

Color can vary widely among species from gray, tawny, or pale brown, to olive, reddish, or dark brown. Some species are solid-colored, but most exhibit characteristic patterns such as dappling, lines or spots, white to brownish or black stripes and bright reddish brown cheeks. The texture of their fur can feel harsh and thin or soft and dense and sometimes woolly.

The most remarkable trait shared by most ground squirrels is they are able to rise up on their hind legs and stand fully erect comfortably for prolonged periods. They can often be seen standing near their burrow entrances searching the territory for predators, when they aren't foraging for food.

Pixabay contributor MrsBrown

Almost all of the ground-dwelling members of the Sciuridae family tend to be gregarious and many live in communities or colonies with complex social structures.

Tree-dwelling squirrels tend to be more solitary than most of their ground-dwelling cousins, although chipmunks are an exception to that rule and rarely live in communities.

During winter, many, but not all types of ground squirrels hibernate in deep underground burrows. They are aroused from winter sleep by spring's warmer temperatures.

Ground squirrels who live in the tropics are active all year and do not store food. Although they sometimes utilize holes in the ground, they usually nest in hollow tree trunks and rotting branches on the forest floor.

Pixabay contributor Skeeze

Most non-tropical ground squirrels are omnivorous. They eat a wide variety of green plant parts, fruits, seeds and grasses as the main part of their diets. Although a few species are not omnivores, many are known to eat insects, caterpillars, ants, crickets, grasshoppers, beetles and their larvae. Some become predators and will go after small vertebrates, such as toads or frogs, and may even invade a bird nest to collect the eggs.

Those living in more tropical or arid environments have adjusted their diets to the types of foods they are most likely to find in their surrounding habitat.

Chipmunks

Chipmunks are small, striped rodents belonging to the family Sciuridae. There are 25 species of chipmunks, living from Canada to Mexico across a variety of habitats from forests to deserts to suburban neighborhoods. Only one species, the Siberian chipmunk, makes its home outside North America, scampering over much of northern Asia. Some chipmunks came to live in Europe when they were introduced via the pet trade in the 1960s. Many escaped or were released when it was discovered that they didn't make very good pets. *It is never a good idea, and in many places illegal, to try to make a pet of any wild creature.*

Chipmunks are small mammals with distinct stripes. Their relatives, the ground squirrel, are often misidentified as a chipmunk. They both have short fur and small ears. The ground squirrel is larger and has a much longer tail. Although a ground squirrel often has body stripes like chipmunks, they never have head stripes.

Colorado chipmunks are medium to large chipmunks. Their central dorsal stripe is black and they have very distinct, dark lateral stripes that are more reddish brown and well-defined white lateral stripes.

Chipmunks are usually found in pinion-juniper woodlands in low elevations and mountain forests at higher elevations. They tend to dwell in the foothills and canyons. They also live in very rocky, broken terrain in woodlands and shrub filled areas.

While some chipmunks make nests in logs or bushes, most prefer to dig vast underground burrows. These hidden homes typically include food storage areas. The sleeping quarters and nesting chamber are kept immaculately clean and lined with leaves and other plant matter. Nut shells and feces are stored in refuse tunnels. These burrows have a several well-concealed, camouflaged entrance holes and the tunnel systems can stretch 10 to 30 feet long.

Like their relatives, the Colorado chipmunks make small vocalizations as it sways its tail from side to side. Whereas the least chipmunk vocalizes while flicking its tail up and down.

Like tree squirrels, Colorado chipmunks are solitary creatures that only get together in the spring during breeding season. The rest of the time they forage for food and form small territories.

Eastern chipmunks mate in early spring and again in early summer, producing litters of four or five young twice each year. Western chipmunks breed only once a year.

Baby chipmunks, which are called kits, kittens or pups, are born blind, hairless and helpless. Imagine something that looks like a pink jelly bean. Pups develop quickly, though. The young emerge from the burrow after about six weeks. They tend to leave the nest and strike out on their own within the next two weeks to make their own way in the world.

Chipmunks tend to forage for food in the early morning and late afternoon. Chipmunks have cheek pouches that allow them to carry more food items in one trip to their burrows for either storage or consumption.

In the wild, chipmunks are omnivores and will feed on a wide variety of foods including seeds, berries, flowers, fungi and other plant material. In lower elevations they feed on juniper "berries" and prickly-pear cactus fruit. They also eat mountain mahogany, currants, wild cherry, and snowberry. Being omnivorous, it is likely that they will eat some types of insects. Chipmunks play an important role as prey for various predatory mammals and birds, but are also opportunistic predators themselves, particularly with regard to worms, small frogs and bird eggs.

Around humans, chipmunks can eat cultivated grains and vegetables, and other plants from farms and gardens, so are often considered pests. Chipmunks mostly forage on the ground, but they can climb trees to obtain nuts such as hazelnuts and acorns.

These small mammals fulfill several important functions in forest ecosystems. Their harvesting and hoarding tree seeds play an inportant role in establishing seedlings in different areas of a forest. They consume many different kinds of fungi and so help to disperse the spores of subterranean truffles which have lost the ability to disperse their spores through the air.

The eastern chipmunk hibernates in the winter, while western chipmunks do not, relying on the stores in their burrows. At the beginning of autumn, many species of chipmunk begin to stockpile nonperishable foods for winter. They mostly cache their foods in a larder inside their burrows and remain in their nests until spring, unlike some other species which make many small caches of food outside their burrows.

Where the name of chipmunk came from.

The name these small mammals are commonly known as may have originally been spelled "chitmunk," derived from the native Ottawa Indian word "jidmoonh", which meant "red squirrel".

Starting in 1842, "chipmonk" was listed in the Oxford English Dictionary. However, "chipmunk" appears in several books from the 1820s and 1830s. Other early forms include "chipmuck" and "chipminck". In the 1830s they were also referred to as "chip squirrels" most likely in reference to the sound they make when chittering about danger. In the mid-1800s, John James Audubon and his sons included a lithograph of the chipmunk in their <u>Viviparous Quadrupeds of North America</u>, in which they called it the "chipping squirrel [or] hackee." Chipmunks have also been referred to as "striped squirrels" and "timber tigers" in various places and times.

Ground Squirrels

The name "ground squirrel" is most often used for the medium-sized ground squirrels, as the larger ones are more commonly known as marmots, woodchucks/groundhogs or prairie dogs. The smaller and less bushy-tailed ground squirrels tend to be known as chipmunks. They are active during the day and have short legs, strong claws, small rounded ears, and a short tail.

Pixabay contributor Chris Chow

They tend to live in open areas including rocky outcrops, fields, pastures, and sparsely wooded hillsides. They also can be found living in grassy areas such as pastures, golf courses, cemeteries, and parks.

Unsplash contributor prashant-saini

Most ground squirrels live up to their names, as they dig burrows and create a system of tunnels underground to live in rather than trees. There is one exception, the California ground squirrel, which lives in a tree.

Pixabay contributor

The main difference between a chipmunk and a ground squirrel is that chipmunks are smaller with distinct stripes, while the tree squirrel is larger and may have body stripes like chipmunks, but they never have head stripes. And some ground squirrels have no stripes whatsoever.

Pixabay contributor

Pixabay contributor cape-xbqs42

All varieties of ground squirrels are renowned for their tendency to rise up on their hind legs. They will do this whenever they sense danger nearby, or when they need to see over tall grasses. When a ground squirrel sees a dangerous predator, it will curl its paws flat against its chest and send a screeching call to warn other family members about the presence of danger.

Pixabay contributor Skeeze

Although ground squirrels look similar to tree squirrels and can climb trees, when frightened they will always retreat to a burrow, whereas tree squirrels will climb a tree or tall structure and never use a burrow. Tree squirrels have no stripes, are larger and have longer tails than ground squirrels.

Pixabay contributor LoggaWiggler

Ground squirrels, like most squirrels, are omnivorous, and will not only eat a diet rich in fungi, nuts, fruits, and seeds, but also occasionally insects, eggs, and other small animals.

Ground squirrels have internal cheek pouches, which they use when gathering food to make fewer trips from the food source back to the burrows where it will be stored.

During winter, ground squirrels hibernate in deep underground burrows. They are aroused from winter sleep by spring's warmer temperatures.

Prairie Dogs

Prairie dogs are named for their habitat and warning call, which sounds similar to a dog's bark. On average, these stout-bodied squirrels will grow to be between 12" to 16" long, including a short tail, and weigh between 1 to 3 lb. The coat of the prairie dog is mottled brown in order to blend in with his surroundings. You will often see prairie dogs sitting up on their haunches. Prairie dogs are found in the western half of North America, stretching from the praries of Canada down to Mexico. As their name implies, they prefer flat land.

Pixabay Public Domain

They are highly social creatures and live in large colonies or "towns". The prairie dog family groups are the most basic units of their society. Members of a family group inhabit the same territory. A prairie dog community is often comprised of many families and can span hundreds of acres.

Prairie dogs live at altitudes ranging from 2,000 to 10,000 ft above sea level. The habitats where they live can get as warm as 100° F in the summer and as cold as −35° F in the winter. Burrows are set up in ways that help prairie dogs control their body temperature to survive the extreme temperatures.

Pixabay contributor Myriams-Fotos

Since prairie dogs tend to live in areas prone to environmental threats, such as hailstorms, blizzards, and floods, as well as drought and prairie fires, their burrows are created in ways to provide important protection. Prairie dog tunnel systems channel rainwater into the water table which prevents runoff and erosion. They can also change the composition of the soil in a region by reversing soil compaction that can result where cattle graze.

Prairie dog burrows range from 16 to 33 feet long and 6.6 to 9.8 feet below the ground. The entrance holes are can be small as 3.9 inches or as large as 11.8 inches in diameter. A prairie dog burrow can have as many six entrances. Some may be flat holes in the ground, others will be surrounded by mounds of soil, either left as piles or hard packed. These mounds serve as observation posts used by the animals to watch for predators. They also protect the burrows from flooding.

Pixabay contributor KevinLindemann

Prairie dog burrows contain chambers to provide certain functions. They have nursery chambers for their young, chambers for night, and chambers for the winter. They also contain air chambers that function to protect the burrow from flooding ,and as a listening post for predators. When hiding from predators, prairie dogs use less-deep chambers that are usually about a foot below the surface.

Prairie dogs are chiefly herbivorous, though they may eat some insects. They feed primarily on various species of grasses and small seeds. In the fall, they will eat broadleaf plants. They also eat roots, seeds, fruit, and buds. Black-tailed prairie dogs in South Dakota eat western bluegrass, buffalo grass, and tumblegrass. Gunnison's prairie dogs primarily eat dandelions, tumbleweeds, saltbush, and cacti in addition to buffalo grass.

Pixabay Public Domain

Prairie dogs are well adapted to protect themselves from predators. Its dichromatic color vision can detect predators from a great distance.

When a predator is spotted they will alert other prairie dogs of the danger with a special, high-pitched call.

Prairie Dog Andy Guez

The most striking of prairie dog communications is their territorial call or "jump-yip" displayed by the black-tailed prairie dog. A black-tailed prairie dog will stretch the length of its body vertically and throw its forefeet into the air while making a call. A jump-yip from one prairie dog causes others nearby to do the same until the whole colony is alerted to potential danger.

Some researchers believe that prairie dogs use a complicated system of vocal communication to describe different predators. It has been suggested that some calls contain information as to which predator it is, how big it is and how fast it is approaching.

Pixabay contributor veronikasz

How they respond varies according to the type of predator that is announced. If the alarm indicates a hawk diving toward the colony, all the prairie dogs in its flight path dive into their holes, while those outside the flight path stand and watch. Coyotes will cause the prairie dogs to move to the entrance of a burrow and stand outside the entrance observing the coyote. Prairie dogs inside the burrows will come out to stand to watch. For domestic dogs, the response is to observe, standing in place where they are when the alarm is sounded, again with the underground prairie dogs emerging to watch. If the alarm is for a human, all members of the colony immediately rush inside the burrows.

Woodchucks / Groundhogs

"Woodchuck" is just another name for "groundhog." Other names that are used for this particular animal include "whistle pig" and "land beaver." The groundhog is one of the 14 species of marmots and is the largest member of the squirrel family. Most marmots live in rocky and mountainous areas, but the woodchuck is a lowland creature. It is often characterized as a ground squirrel that can climb trees and swim in water.

Pixabay contributor Skeeze

Woodchucks can grow to be as long as twenty-six inches and weigh up to nine pounds. They are built for digging with short, powerful limbs and curved, thick claws. They have heavy-duty claws and thickly muscled forearms. They differ from other Sciuridaes because their spine is slightly rounded. Their coat is grayish brown and has two layers for extra insulation during the winter months. Unlike other squirrels, the tail of a groundhog very short, only about one-fourth of their body length.

Woodchucks like all rodents have large incisor teeth. Their four incisors will grow 1/16 of an inch per week, but constant usage wears them down by about that much each week. While the groundhog may not threaten you or your pets, if their burrow is invaded, the groundhog will tenaciously defend itself with its large incisors and wickedly sharp front claws.

Pixabay contributor dreamstime_Murmeltier

Groundhogs are common in most North American areas such as Canada and the United States, including Alaska. Groundhogs don't require the same amount of flat prairie that their cousins, the prairie dogs, need to live comfortably. Unlike their fellow marmots, they are lowland creatures with short but powerful limbs and curved, thick claws for digging. Their spine is curved, and they have two coats of fur. They are also equipped with two very large incisors.

Groundhogs do live in burrows, but not in huge colonies like prairie dogs. At the most, three or four groundhogs will occupy the same burrow. Groundhogs are territorial among their own species, and may engage in short fights to establish dominance.

Pixabay contributor Linnaea Mallette

Thier burrows are most often established along forest edges near open fields like meadows, besides roads or near streams.

Similar to the prairie dog burrow, a groundhog's burrow has a number of entrances and exits, to give it a good way to escape from predators.

A Tongue Twister By Mother Goose
How much wood could a woodchuck chuck
If a woodchuck could chuck wood?
As much wood as a woodchuck could chuck,
If a woodchuck could chuck wood.

Groundhogs are mostly herbivorous, and primarily eat wild grasses and other vegetation. An adult woodchuck will eat more than a pound of vegetation daily. In some areas they are considered as garden pests, since their diet consists mostly of plants like grass, fruits, berries, agricultural crops, and tree bark.

Pixabay contributor Iggy 7117

In early spring they enjoy munching on dandelions and coltsfoot. Some additional foods include sheep sorrel, agrimony, timothy grass, buttercup, red and black raspberries, buckwheat, plantain, wild lettuce, all varieties of clover, and alfalfa. Occasionally they will eat grubs, grasshoppers, insects, snails and other small animals, but are not as omnivorous as many other members of this species.

They don't seem to drink much water, and are believed to obtain needed liquids from the juices of food plants, aided by their sprinkling with rain or dew.

When outside their burrows and not actively feeding, they may appear nearly motionless, standing erect on their hind feet watching for danger. A high-pitched whistle from a groundhog outside of a burrow is an indication of an incoming predator and danger. The groundhog can also produce other sounds, like low barks or a sound produced by grinding its teeth.

Groundhogs may hide when they see, smell or hear a nearby observer. Burrows are used for their protection from predators, such as wolves, coyotes, foxes, bobcats, bears, hawks, owls, and dogs. Although they prefer to retreat to their burrows when threatened, they have also been seen climbing trees or swimming to escape predators.

Pixabay contributor Linnaea Mallette

An unusual trait of groundhogs is that they are one of the few animals that undergo complete hibernation during the winter. Many will build a separate "winter burrow" for this purpose. This burrow is usually in a wooded or brushy area and is dug below the frost line and maitains a stable temperature, well above freezing, during the winter months.

In early autumn, a groundhog's metabolism slows, food intake decreases, their weight increases by as much as 100%. They produce fat deposits that they will live upon during hibernation all winter. Winter comes in some of their habitats as early as October and usually lasts until the start of Spring in late March or early April. When winter arrives, they escape to their burrows, curl into a ball, slow their heartbeat and lower their body temperature to sleep until spring.

Pixabay contributor Linnaea Mallette

When spring arrives they awake and it signifies new life for the groundhogs when a litter of six newborns is usually born.

Pixabay contributor pizano13

Groundhog Day is a popular tradition celebrated in the United States and Canada on February 2nd. It derives from a Pennsylvania Dutch legend. If a groundhog emerges from its burrow on this day and sees his shadow due to clear weather, it will retreat to its den and winter will persist for six more weeks. If it does not see its shadow because of cloudiness, spring will arrive early. While the tradition remains popular in modern times, studies have found no consistent correlation between a groundhog seeing its shadow or not and the subsequent arrival time of spring-like weather.

Marmots

Marmots are another member of the squirrel family. There 14 species of these very large ground squirrels. They inhabit plains and open country in mountainous regions in North America, the European Alps, north-central Asia, the Himalayas, and northeastern Siberia to the Kamchatka Peninsula. They tend to live in open country in mountains and plains, preferring mountain meadows, steppes, tundra, and forest edges.

Pixabay contributor Mrs. Brown

Marmots have been known since antiquity. Fossils of marmots have been found in North America as far back as 13.8 million years ago.

The typical marmot has a rather short tail. They all are large and heavy squirrels, weighing from 6.6 to 15.4 pounds, depending upon the species. The alpine marmot is the largest living member of the Sciuridae family.

Pixabay contributor jehyun-sung

They are well suited for life in cold environments and have small fur-covered ears, short, stocky legs, and strong claws for digging. Their long, thick fur is slightly coarse and may be yellowish brown, often frosted with buff white, brown, reddish brown, black, or a mixture of gray and white. Unlike most other members of the squirrel family they have a short, bushy tail.

Marmots typically live in burrows that they excavate. Most mountain species construct burrows beneath boulder fields, rocky slopes, and crevices in cliff faces. This terrain provides protection from predators such as grizzly bears, which are aggressive diggers and a significant predator of the Alaska marmot. They use cliffs as observation sites where they will sit upright watching for both terrestrial and aerial predators. When alarmed, marmots emit a sharp, piercing whistle and scurry to their burrows if danger persists.

Pixabay Public Domain

Marmots are active during the day and are almost entirely vegetarian. They eat mostly greens and many types of grasses, berries, lichens, mosses, roots, and flowers.

Aside from the fact that they may be eating your plants, marmots are not all that dangerous, preferring to lounge around all day. The most dangerous thing about marmots is that they can carry some nasty things like ticks that cause Lyme disease, or Rocky Mountain Spotted Fever.

Pixabay contributor Pixel-mixer

Most marmots are highly social and some species live in large colonies, but none as large as a prairie dog community.

All hibernate in winter, most of them deeply underground, although some may emerge from their burrows for short periods on mild winter days. During hibernation they live on fat reserves accumulated during the summer. And in the Spring the young are born.

Predators

Pixabay contributor DaFranzosy

All species of squirrels have many natural enemies. Lynxes, bobcats, coyotes, foxes, wolves, weasels, great horned owls, hawks, and even the American crow hunt them.

Unsplash contributor vincent-van-zalinge

Unsplash contributor brian-kraus

Although an adult squirrel can live as long as five, or even ten years in the wild, sadly, most squirrels will die in their first year of life. Falling prey to a predator is the most common cause for a ground squirrel's death.

Their natural enemies exist on the ground and in the sky and are always searching for their next meal.

Unsplash contributor harsh-tank

As a free bonus you can find a free PDF to download with a simple word search and crossword puzzle using a few of the glossary words at:
www.hierographicsbooksllc.com/squirrels-bonus/

Or you may chose to access a little PDF booklet that has more word searches and crossword puzzles using the words in the glossary, plus it includes a few squirrel poems with simple illustrations and a squirrelly maze.

Discover the World of Squirrels Bonus from HieroGraphics Books LLC

Discover more books published by HieroGraphics Books at:

www.HieroGraphicsBooksLLC.com

Do you have a book you want to write? Or have one written?
We help people get their books published.
Visit the web site to learn more!

Photographic Images by Julia L. Wright ©2015
HieroGraphics Books © 2019

Ground Squirrel Glossary

adapts (adapted): to change a behavior so that it is easier to live in a particular place or situation.

adorable: cute, charming, delightful, enchanting, captivating.

agriculture: the science or practice of farming, including cultivation of the soil for growing crops and the raising of animals to provide food, wool, and other products.

agricultural: relating to agriculture.

ancestor: a person or group from whom an individual, group, or species has descended.

arid: a very dry climate with very little rain, sparse vegetation or where few animals can survive; desert.

breeding: the mating of animals to create offspring.

burrow (n): a tunnel or hole dug by an animal where they live.
burrow (v): to dig a hole or tunnel in the earth.

caches: places for hiding, storing, or preserving treasure or supplies.

camouflage: to hide, conceal or disguise the existence of a person, object or animal; make it appear to be part of the natural surroundings by covering it up in ways it matches its environment.

characteristic: a quality or feature belongingn typically to a person, place, or thing that serves to identify it.

colony: a group of individuals living closely together.

community: a group of individuals living together in same area.

complex: complicated; group of many connected and different parts.

consume (consumption): to drink, eat, use up, destroy or take in food, beverages, time or goods.

den: where a wild animal has hollowed out a living space.

desert (v): to withdraw from, abandon or leave without intent to return; leaving a space empty and no longer occupied or used.

desert (n): very dry land with very little vegetation and sparse amounts of water.

dichromatic: a form of color-blindness in which only two light wavelengths are distinguished rather than the usual three. *Helps to experience better vision in dim light.*

diverse: exhibiting varied or different characteristics or unlike qualities.

ecosystem: all the plants and animals that are interconnected by living in a specific area.

environment: the surrounding conditions or forces that influence or modify the whole complex of factors, as soil, climate, and plants and animals that influence the form and the ability of a plant or animal or ecological community to survive.

excavate: to dig a hole or tunnel in the earth.

exception: does not follow a rule or is different from others of its kind.

feces: solid waste matter discharged from the bowels after food has been digested.

forage (foraging): to search a wide area for food.

fossil: naturally preserved remains or traces of animals or plants that lived in the geologic past, usually seen in rocks.

fungi (fungus): any of a kingdom of living things (as molds, rusts, mildews, smuts, and mushrooms) that lack chlorophyll.

genus: a category of classification in biology that ranks between the family and the species: contains related species, and is named by a capitalized noun formed in Latin.

gregarious: people or animals that are very social and enjoy being in crowds or large groups.

grind (grinding): to reduce to small fragments by friction with the teeth.

habitat: the place or type of area where a plant or animal naturally or normally lives or grows.

hibernate (hibernation): to spend the winter in a dormant state or sleep through the winter.

hibernation: being in a deep state of sleep during the winter.

hoard: keep a supply of something valuable hidden and guarded for future use.

incisors: a front tooth for cutting; especially one of the cutting teeth between the canines of a mammal.

irresistible: impossible to resist.

kits: baby squirrels or chipmunks.

larder: a place where food is stored for future use.

litter: a group of young animals born at the same time.
litter: trash that is left outside trash cans that causes harm to the environment and is a danger to animals.

mammal: warm-blooded higher vertebrates that nurse their young with milk and have skin that is usually, but not always covered with hair. (Humans are mammals.)

mound: rounded hill or pile of dirt.

native: born in a particular place or country; grown, produced, or having its beginning in a particular region.

nonperishable: won't spoil, rot, decay or become inedible over a long time in storge.

omnivore: a type of animal that feeds on both animal and vegetable substances.
omnivorous: feeds on both animal and vegetable substances.

pests: troublesome, annoying, or destructive animal or insect that destroys garden plants or farm crops .

posturing: to take a particular posture, stance or pose.

predator: an animal that hunts a smaller or weaker animal for food.

primarily: for the most part, chiefly, in the first place, originally.

rain forest: a densely wooded forest area that has consistent heavy rainfall, usually in a tropical location.

remarkable: unusual, extraordinary, special or distinguishing.

repertoire: the stock of special skills, devices, techniques of a particular person, an animal or a particular field of endeavor.

residential: an area or part of a town where many homes exist.

Rodent: a relatively small gnawing mammal with very sharp, constantly growing incisors. They make up the largest order of mammals and exist on all continents except Antarctica.

scamper: to run or move quickly, often in a very playfully and happy looking manner.

Sciuridae: mammal family of true squirrels.

semi-arid: an area with very little rainfall and usually has very hot temperatures, where plants and animals struggle to exist.

solitary: growing or living alone; not forming part of a group.

species: a class of things of the same kind and with the same name; a category of living things that ranks below a genus, and is made up of related individuals able to produce fertile offspring, and is identified by a two-part scientific name.

storage: a place where items are kept available for future use.

subfamily: a phylogentic subdivision, of more importance than genus, into which certain families are divided; small group of animals within a species/family.

subterranean: occurring, lying or existing under the earth's surface, such as a tunnel.

suburban: relating to a housing area near a big city.

temperate: a moderate climate that is found in the earth's middle latitudes. Usually a climate that has four season, but rarely has extreme temperatures.

terrain: the physical features of a piece of land in a specific geographic area.

territorial: the protection of an area in which an animal lives.

trait: distinguishing characteristic.

tropics (tropical): relating to a very warm climate near the equator.

typical: distinctive qualities of a specific thing.

urban: describes an area where humans live in a city.

vegetation: plants that cover a certain habitat.

vocal: producing sounds using a mouth.

vocalizations: the act, process, or instance of creating vocal sounds.

As a bonus lesson, you can find a free PDF to download with a simple word search and crossword puzzle using some glossary words at:
www.hierographicsbooksllc.com/squirrels-bonus/

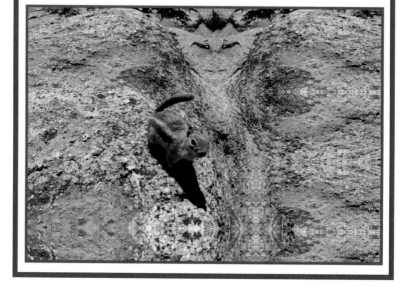

FREE Discover Squirrels Glossary Bonus from HieroGraphics Books LLC

Or you may chose to access a little PDF booklet that has more word searches and a crossword puzzle using the words in the glossary, plus it includes a few squirrel poems with simple illustrations and a squirrelly maze. Go to:
www.hierographicsbooksllc.com/squirrels-bonus/
to discover both bonus offerings.

Discover the World of Squirrels Bonus
from HieroGraphics Books LLC

If you enjoyed this book and haven't seen
the original book about tree squirrels
"Discover the World of Squirrels"
it can be found on Amazon at:
http://www.amazon.com/dp/1512255335/
On Amazon, do a Search for "HieroGraphics Books" and you
will find more books and journals created by Julia L. Wright.
*There are also and mugs with squirrel images to delight you or
a favorite child that loves squirrels.*

On ETSY, in the author's FantaFaces Store, there are decks of
playing cards with squirrel and wildflower images that kids
love to play with! *And some of the mugs are listed there also.*
https://www.etsy.com/shop/Fantafaces

Made in the USA
Columbia, SC
06 July 2021

41497478R00035